A Guide to
CATHOLIC
WEDDINGS

Q&A for Couples

SANDRA DOOLEY

LITURGY
TRAINING
PUBLICATIONS

Nihil Obstat
Very Reverend Daniel A. Smilanic, JCD
Vicar for Canonical Services
Archdiocese of Chicago
April 4, 2016

Imprimatur
Very Reverend Ronald A. Hicks
Vicar General
Archdiocese of Chicago
April 4, 2016

The *Nihil Obstat* and *Imprimatur* are official declarations that a book is free of doctrinal and moral error. No implication is contained therein that those who have granted the *Nihil Obstat* and *Imprimatur* agree with the content, opinions, or statements expressed. Nor do they assume any legal responsibility associated with publication.

This book was edited by Danielle A. Noe, MDIV. Christopher Magnus was the production editor, Anna Manhart was the designer, and Kari Nicholls was the production artist.

Cover and interior art © Martin Erspamer, OSB.

20 19 18 17 16   1 2 3 4 5

Printed in the United States of America.

Library of Congress Control Number: 2016938244

ISBN 978-1-61671-238-9

GCW

Contents

Introduction

Dear Bride and Groom,

Congratulations! In a few months you will embark on the journey of a life-long partnership with the one you love. This journey began when you first met and became attracted to each other, and it will hopefully continue through many years of mutual happiness and love—your love for each other, for God, for your family and friends, and all God's people.

Marriage, or Matrimony, is one of the seven sacraments of the Catholic Church. The sacraments mark special moments and celebrate the presence of God in our lives. In the Sacrament of Matrimony the two of you will promise to be true to each other and to love and honor each other for the rest of your lives. It is the formal, official beginning of your life together as a married couple. And, if you really think about it, the way you live out your vows and grow in faith and in love in your daily lives is even more important than the actual ceremony in which you become husband and wife.

The Catholic Bishops of the United States say:

> A committed, permanent, faithful relationship of husband and wife is the root of a family. It strengthens all the members, provides best for the needs of children, and causes the church of the home to be an effective sign of Christ in the world.[1]

As you begin preparing for your wedding in the Catholic Church, there are some things you need to do as a couple. That's what this

---

1   *Follow the Way of Love: A Pastoral Message of the U.S. Catholic Bishops to Families on the Occasion of the United Nations 1994 International Year of the Family*, p. 11.

book is about. In it you will find questions (and answers) about various steps you need to take in order to prepare for and celebrate your Catholic wedding, from the start of your engagement until after the last note of the recessional is played. Some aspects of your preparation will depend on the priest or deacon who will be officiating at your wedding or on the customs of the parish in which your wedding will take place, but there are other elements that are common to all Catholic weddings in the world.

Please know that as you prepare for your wedding, and a lifetime of mutual and self-sacrificing love, in addition to your family and friends, you have the support of the Church: those who are involved in your preparation as well as people in the parish who will be praying for you. Your Marriage is important to you as a couple, but also to the entire Church as a symbol of the love that Jesus Christ has for all his people.

This book will help you understand the Roman Catholic Marriage ceremony and the rules surrounding its celebration. This resource presents Catholic teaching about the Catholic Marriage ritual and is intended to answer your questions and explain the requirements, expectations, and joys of getting married in the Catholic Church. In the pages of this book, along with answers to many of your questions, you will find ideas and suggestions to help you in asking questions of the priest, deacon, or parish wedding coordinator as you go through the preparation process. You will also find mention of other resources which might be available through your parish, online, or in a Catholic bookstore. This book will help you prepare a truly sacred ceremony, one that reflects your love for God and your love for each other.

You may want to keep this book handy during the next several months, so that you can consult it as questions arise.

May God bless you both as you embark on this wonderful journey into a long and happy married life, growing together in faith and in love.

—Sandra Dooley

Marriage Preparation in the Catholic Church

1. We have just become engaged and would like to have a Catholic wedding. What do we need to do first?

Congratulations on your engagement! You have already made the first of many important decisions in your life together as a couple. This is an important step in preparing for your wedding, and one that shows the importance of the Catholic faith in your life.

The first thing to do is pick up a parish bulletin when you go to church for Mass next Sunday, and look for information about Catholic weddings. Most parishes publish this information in the bulletin along with the name of the contact person including their phone number and/or e-mail address. The contact person may vary—it may be the pastor, deacon, music or liturgy director, wedding coordinator, or even the parish secretary. Oftentimes there is also a page on the parish website devoted to sacramental preparation.

When you are ready to set the date and make formal arrangements with the parish, call and make an appointment with the appropriate person on the parish staff. If you call the main office number listed in the bulletin, the parish secretary should be able to connect you with the appropriate person.

It is very important that you speak with someone at the parish *before* you set a date and/or put a deposit down on a reception hall. The parish staff will be very happy to help schedule your ceremony and contacting them first will save you headaches down the road—especially with potential scheduling conflicts between the parish and your reception venue.

Many parishes provide a small booklet or handout outlining parish policies and procedures for weddings. This booklet is often made available on the parish website. You can ask about this when you call.

Some parishes also require that you be a registered parishioner for a certain amount of time before you can set a date and begin preparations for your Church wedding. The amount of time may vary from as little as three months to as long as twelve months, so it would be a good idea for at least one of you to register in your parish right now (if you are not already a registered parishioner) and begin to make yourself known to the pastor or someone on the parish staff.

When you decide to get married in the Catholic Church, the expectation is that you are not just choosing a venue for your wedding, but you are choosing to celebrate as a member of this particular Catholic Christian community. "Venues" are chosen for the reception and for the rehearsal dinner. Your Marriage in a Catholic church expresses and symbolizes your participation in the life of that parish and the faith community that surrounds you with their loving support and prayers. The priest or deacon who officiates (presides) at your Catholic wedding is an official representative of the Catholic Church. He receives and witnesses your mutual consent in the name of the Church and extends to you the blessing of the Church.

2. We are not members of a parish but would like to get married in the Catholic Church. Is this allowed?

Yes, although many parishes require that you are registered for several months before beginning your Marriage preparation. When you have a Catholic wedding, you are choosing to exchange your vows (or consent) within a particular Catholic community. Ideally, the parish in which you profess your wedding vows is the faith community in which you usually worship, and which has the responsibility to support you and pray for you as you begin your married life.

If you are not registered in a parish, consider having your wedding ceremony in a parish with which you have some connection. Perhaps you attend Mass regularly in this parish, your parents are parishioners there, or you and your family have some historical ties to the parish. It is not a good reason to choose a church for your wedding just because it is "pretty" or because it is close to the place where you want to have your reception. The Catholic Church wants to support you in your commitment to each other, and wants you to be an active member of the faith community.

As mentioned earlier, most parishes require that you be registered for several months before beginning your Marriage preparation, which itself could last six to twelve months. This assures the pastor and others that you are serious about getting married as a Catholic and that you are actively practicing your faith. This is even more important when getting married somewhere other than your home parish.

The procurement of all the necessary documents will probably take longer and be a little more complicated than usual since several parishes may be involved.

3. Why should we consider registering at a local parish?

As noted in questions #1 and #2, some parishes do require that you become a registered parishioner. Involvement in a parish community is important for our life of faith. As a sacrament, Marriage is a public ceremony or a public act of worship of the Church, called liturgy.[1] Even though you may send wedding invitations to family and friends, the ceremony really belongs to the entire Church. When you become a member of a Catholic parish community, you belong to the universal Catholic Church. And it is through the Church that you are able to experience or become closer to Christ through the celebration of the sacraments:

> The parish is where the Church lives. Parishes are communities of faith, of action, and of hope. They are where the Gospel is proclaimed and celebrated, where believers are formed and sent to renew the earth. Parishes are the home of the Christian community; they are the heart of our Church. Parishes are the place where God's people meet Jesus in word and sacrament and come in touch with the source of the Church's life.[2]

The members of your parish community, as part of the Body of Christ, are visible signs of Christ's love for us. When we worship together—even at the wedding ceremony—we are one with each other. The parish community is where we learn about Christ, where we

---

1   See also page 20, question 1, for a more thorough treatment on the meaning of Catholic liturgy.

2   *Communities of Salt and Light*, p. 1.

express what we believe, and where we go forth to serve God in our world. We do this together in faith. When you choose to be married in the Catholic Church, the parish community will pray for you, share in your joy, and welcome you as a married couple committed to living Christian lives of faith.

Just as important as registering in a parish is regular attendance at worship, when you share the Eucharist with other Catholic Christians. You will hear about and participate in many social events and opportunities for spiritual reflection. Many friendships are formed as a result of your participation in parish events. This makes attendance at Mass more of a complete experience of community, because you actually know some of the people with whom you are worshipping. In fact, you probably look forward to seeing them each Sunday. You can then share with them any good news that you may have, for example, that you are looking forward to your first baby. People enjoy the opportunity to share your joy and you enjoy having people around who genuinely care about you.

It is in the parish that you will marry, that you will raise your children in the faith, that you will form lasting friendships, and receive support in both your spiritual and personal lives.

Registering at a local parish is quite simple. Information is usually printed in the parish bulletin and posted on the parish website. You can also call the main office at your parish, and the parish staff will be able to help you.

4. Our parents are encouraging us to have a Catholic wedding, but we are uncertain. Why should we choose to have a Catholic wedding rather than have a civil ceremony?

Parents want the best for their children, and hope that their adult children have embraced their values. The Catholic faith may be very important to your parents, and they may want you to celebrate your Marriage in the Church as a sign of your faithfulness to Christ and to the core values they have tried to impart to you over the years. When you get married in the Church, you are affirming your faith and belief in Jesus Christ. You may also be showing a certain amount of respect for your parents and for their faith that they hold so dear. For many adults, faith grows deeper as they get older. Your parents probably understand the importance of their faith much more now than they did when they were first married, and they want the same for you!

Marriage, or Matrimony, is a sacrament in the Catholic Church and when you celebrate your Marriage in the Church you invite Christ into your lives to nourish and sustain your mutual love and to give you the grace and strength (God's presence) to live out the promises you make throughout the many days of your married life. That may not seem to be a challenge now, when you are both feeling deeply in love, but as the years go on, you will rely on that grace and strength—God's presence—to carry you through whatever difficulties may arise in your relationship and in your lives.

5. Why is Marriage considered a sacrament?

The sacraments of the Catholic Church are the primary ways in which we encounter God's grace, become one with Christ, and strengthen our relationship with God and each other. Participating in the sacraments, especially the weekly (or daily) celebration of the Eucharist, helps us to be more like Christ. There are seven sacraments in the Church and many of them are celebrated at significant moments in the life of the individual. For example, Baptism celebrates our new life in Christ and the fact that we are children of God. Confirmation is a celebration of the coming and presence of the Holy Spirit in our lives, and Reconciliation heals our broken relationship with God.

The Church teaches that "the purpose of the sacraments is to sanctify people, to build up the body of Christ, and, finally, to worship God."[3] When you get married, your life together will symbolize the love of Christ for his Church. This is evident in your deep and self-sacrificing love for each other. As baptized Christians, you

---

3   *Constitution on the Sacred Liturgy*, 59.

invite Christ into your relationship and rely on him to give both of you the strength and commitment needed to live together as a married couple. The Church teaches that when you celebrate the Sacrament of Matrimony in the Church, you experience God's grace—his presence—in in a special way. Your Marriage symbolizes God's great love for his people. This love is revealed through Christ himself. And it is Christ himself who blesses your union.

In a sacramental Marriage, the two of you freely consent and affirm that yours is a mutual, loving relationship in which you promise lifelong fidelity. Before God and the whole Church (represented by your family, friends, and others present) you declare your love for each other and the fact that you are open to having children together (if possible). These promises are received by a representative of the Catholic Church, almost always a priest or a deacon, who then blesses your union in the name of the Church. Your Marriage is recognized by the Church and is supported and sustained by the members of the Church who surround you not only on the day of your wedding but throughout the years of your Marriage.

In order for Marriage to be considered a sacrament, it must take place between two baptized Christians who have come by their own free will, without impediments (such as a previous marriage), to marry in the Church. The couple must freely consent to marry with the intention of a life-long commitment as well as being open to life. The Marriage must be validly celebrated (that is, the wedding follows the Catholic ritual), and a priest or deacon and two additional witnesses (the witnesses are usually the maid [or matron] of honor and the best man) must witness the couples' exchange of consent to marry. Although a marriage between a Catholic and a person who is not baptized may be validly celebrated, it is not considered sacramental. In order for a sacramental Marriage to take place, both parties must be baptized. An unconsummated marriage is not considered validly celebrated and is, therefore, not considered to be a sacrament.

6. If we choose to get married civilly at the local court house, what does that mean for us as Catholics?

Since Marriage is a sacrament, Catholics are expected to publicly celebrate their Marriage in a Catholic ceremony and have their vows (giving of consent) officially received by a priest or deacon.

If a Marriage takes place in front of a justice of the peace or another civil authority, it is not considered to be a sacramental Marriage. Because the Marriage is not considered a sacramental Marriage, the Church does not recognize that the Marriage has taken place. Because of this, a couple may no longer receive Communion.

If a couple has married civilly and wishes for their Marriage to be considered sacramental, they must express their consent (share their vows) and promise their fidelity to one another in a Catholic ceremony. This ceremony is called "convalidation" and it involves the giving of consent and exchange of promises in order for the marriage to be considered a sacrament. It can be done in the presence of family and friends either at Mass or outside of Mass. If one of the spouses in such a marriage has been previously married and has not received an annulment of their earlier marriage, the convalidation cannot take place.[4] He or she will need to go through the process of applying for an annulment before entering into another sacramental Marriage in the Church. If you are in such a situation, it is best to talk with your priest or another staff member who can discuss your particular situation, and walk you through the annulment process if necessary.

---

4   An annulment is the official recognition by the Church that a marriage was not sacramental. Those who were previously married and have been divorced and wish to remarry in the Catholic Church must disclose this information to their pastor in order to determine if one is free to marry within the Church. The United States Conference of Catholic Bishops provides on their website a very helpful resource regarding annulments: www.foryourmarriage.org/catholic-marriage/church-teachings/annulments/.

7. It is a custom in our home country to have both a civil ceremony and a religious ceremony. Is it done this way in the United States?

In some countries, civil authorities are the only ones who can declare a legal marriage between two people. However, Catholic priests and deacons are recognized as official witnesses of Marriage in the United States. Therefore, there is no need to have a separate civil ceremony.

If you have been married civilly (either in the United States or another country) and want your marriage to be considered a sacrament, your pastor or someone on the parish staff can help you with the proper procedures and preparation for convalidation.

8. With whom at the parish church do we need to meet in order to have a Catholic wedding? What will they require?

As with many other aspects of preparing for your Marriage, the answer to this question will vary from parish to parish, depending on the pastor, the size of the parish, and/or the expertise and distribution of responsibilities of people on the parish staff or the requirements of the diocese.

Every parish belongs to a diocese, which governs certain aspects of parish life, under the leadership of a bishop. Dioceses have different policies regarding preparation for Marriage, so it is best to find out well ahead of time what the requirements are in your local diocese as well as in the diocese in which you will be married.

Generally speaking, you need to start by calling the parish office and letting them know you wish to speak with someone about getting married in the church. In some parishes, the director of liturgy meets with engaged couples and works with them throughout the process. In other parishes, there may be another staff member or wedding coordinator (or even the pastor himself) who will guide you through the process. Most parishes require a minimum of six months' notice and preparation time for weddings. Some parishes require a year. This length of time is needed to complete all your paperwork, and to allow time for Marriage preparation programs. In some large and/or very busy parishes, weddings are scheduled a year or more in advance.

At some point, hopefully early in the process, you will meet with the pastor of the parish where you will be getting married, or with the priest who will officiate (preside) at your wedding ceremony. Engaged couples are expected to participate in a pre-Marriage program, such as Pre-Cana, Unitas, or Engaged Encounter. Additionally, many parishes provide a sponsor couple for every couple preparing for Marriage. Your sponsor couple may work with you and/or accompany you through whatever process your parish follows as you prepare for your wedding. All of this takes place over a period of several months, so the earlier you make the initial contact, the better.

Well before the wedding you will need to consult with the parish liturgist or musician. This is the person who will work with you and advise you about the choice of music, cantors, and other musicians. Practices vary from parish to parish. Some parishes do not permit anyone else to play for weddings other than parish staff. Other parishes welcome guest musicians and/or expect you to find your own musicians. If you are concerned about the quality of the music at your wedding, it would be wise to speak with the parish musician and make arrangements as early as possible (six months or more before the wedding). Again, the sooner the better.

In some parishes, the liturgist or director of music schedules wedding workshops at certain times throughout the year. All couples who are preparing to get married in that parish are required to attend these workshops. At these workshops, the liturgist or music director will teach you about the Catholic wedding ceremony, discuss the many options for the ceremony, and provide music samples from which to choose. If you're unsure if your parish offers these workshops, it is best to call the parish office.

9. What will the meeting with the pastor be like? What questions will he ask?

Of course, every pastor is different, but there are some basic things that the pastor will want to discuss with you. Be prepared for the pastor to ask many sensitive questions and consider your responses beforehand. He will want to get to know both of you, if he doesn't know you already. He will want to know that you are coming regularly to Mass on weekends. He will also want to know if either of you have been married before, why you want to get married, if both of you are Catholic, if you both have been baptized, and if you are living together.

The pastor will also hopefully take some time to simply visit with you. He will want to have a sense of how mature your relationship is, and how much you agree or disagree on important issues such as money and children. Most dioceses require the completion of some type of questionnaire or premarital inventory to help determine how close your feelings and beliefs are about significant life issues (in some dioceses, this inventory is called FOCCUS). Your pastor, or whoever is working with you, will coordinate the taking of the questionnaire. The results will help guide at least some of your conversations with him.

All of these things serve to give your pastor, or whoever is working with you, a sense of how important your Catholic faith is and that it will continue to be an integral part of your lives. Fortunately for you, when you come to the Catholic Church to be married, you are getting so much more than someone to officiate (preside) at your wedding! Through the preparation process you will be accompanied by one or more people, who care about your relationship and want to help it grow and flourish, rooted in the love of Jesus Christ.

10. What materials or documents do we need to provide our parish in order to have a Catholic wedding?

You will each need to submit a certificate of Baptism (if both of you are baptized) by the parish where you were baptized to help ensure that no previous marriage has taken place. Some parishes also require Confirmation and first Communion certificates, although that information should be included with the baptismal certificate.

It is also common practice for each of you to provide forms from two witnesses—either from parents, other close relatives, or friends who have known you for a designated period of time. These forms (called "affidavits") state that you are free to marry, and that you are not getting married against your will. In most circumstances, the witnesses will need to sign the affidavits in the presence of a priest or deacon.

Your parish will probably provide a prenuptial questionnaire for each of you to fill out giving information such as the date and place of your Baptism and Confirmation, length of your relationship, assurance that there are no impediments to a sacramental Marriage, and that you both intend to be faithful for life.[5]

In some cases you may be required to submit other documents such as a dispensation from a previous marriage (a statement that you are free to marry again), a certificate of death of a previous spouse, or documentation about another irregular or unusual situation.

Prior to the ceremony itself, you will also need to supply the marriage license. This is for legal purposes and each state and/or county has different rules and time frames for acquiring the license. Your parish will be able to help you acquire the license.

Your parish should provide a list of everything that is needed, and perhaps even give you a checklist to keep track of what you have turned in and what documents are still outstanding.

---

5 Examples of impediments include: a previous marriage that has not been annulled, lack of openness to having children, a man who is still bound by the vows of priesthood, and a person who has taken a vow of perpetual chastity.

When you approach the parish in a timely manner (six or more months before the intended date of your wedding) you usually have time to gather this information. A word to the wise, however; begin requesting and collecting the necessary documents as soon as possible so that you don't run into any last minute delays, particularly if you are gathering documents from other dioceses or even other countries. You don't want to find yourself scrambling to acquire essential documents in the last few weeks leading up to your wedding. You'll have plenty of other things to concern yourself with at that point! The only document you don't want to request too soon is your baptismal certificate. It is often required that the baptismal certificate be issued within six months of your wedding date. If you don't remember the name of the church where you were baptized, check with your parents or other relatives who may have been present at your Baptism. If all else fails, try contacting someone at the diocesan office closest to where you were born. They may be able to guide you in figuring out where you were baptized, or help you locate the records of a parish that may have closed. You can typically look online to get contact information for a diocese. Most, if not all, dioceses in the United States now have websites. If you are not sure about the city or name of the diocese, get in touch with a church in the general area and ask in what diocese that parish is located.

11. We live in Illinois but we're going to be married in another state where our family lives. Where do we do our wedding preparations?

It will probably be more convenient for you to do your Marriage preparations where you live. You will need to work with your local priest (who will want some assurance that you are attending Sunday Mass). Your local parish can arrange for the necessary interviews and other aspects of preparation. If you are not a member of a parish, you should call a Catholic church in your local area. The parish staff will be able to help you. However, you and/or your local parish will need to be in touch with your family's parish to make sure that what is acceptable in your own diocese is also acceptable in your family's diocese.

It is important for you to make contact personally with the parish where you plan to be married and hopefully schedule an early meeting with the priest or deacon who will officiate (or preside) at the ceremony. This should all be done many months before the wedding so that you can be sure you are complying with all the policies of the parish and diocese in which you will celebrate your Marriage. You will also want to find out what the parish policies are regarding music, musicians, and other aspects of the ceremony. Be sure to talk or communicate with someone at the parish yourself. Most parishes will not schedule a wedding at the request of a third party (for example, your mother or a close friend). It is you—the bride and groom—who are the key persons in this situation and who need to be in direct contact with the parish and the priest or deacon who will officiate (preside) at your Marriage. Wherever you prepare for your Marriage, it is important that you do so as a couple.

12. Why is Marriage preparation required?

The many dioceses in the United States have different policies about Marriage preparation for engaged couples. There are a variety of pre-Marriage preparation programs, including Pre-Cana, Engaged Encounter, Unitas, and others. All of them have the same goal: to help both of you prepare for your life together after Marriage, and to ensure that there is "a living faith and fruitful love"[6] between the two of you. The Church wants your Marriage to be successful and to last for the rest of your lives. The Church also wants some assurance that the two of you will make every effort to live out your love in the light of your Catholic faith.

All of us are familiar with couples whose marriages have broken down in one way or another, many times due to the fact that the couple discovered serious differences in their values, lifestyles,

---

6   *The Order of Celebrating Matrimony,* 20. This source is the official ritual book of the Church that governs the celebration of the wedding ceremony.

or priorities *after* getting married. These programs help ensure that both of you are very aware of each other's positions and values in various areas of life, and help you assess your compatibility in those areas. Even though you may feel such programs are unnecessary for you, the Church expects that you will make an honest effort to participate—to provide some assurance to those working with you that you really want this Marriage to work, and that you are committed to each other in a faith-filled loving relationship for the rest of your lives.

These programs also offer ways of dealing with difficulties that arise in relationships, including any serious issues that might be a threat to your relationship in future years.

Natural Family Planning (NFP) classes are required to make sure that Catholic couples are familiar with the teachings of the Church on sexuality and the openness to the gift of life in your relationship.

Try to make the most of these opportunities. You will surely find them to have a positive effect on your relationship. Participation in these preparation programs assures that you have discussed and reached consensus on all the important areas of agreement needed to ensure a successful transition to married life.

13. Do we have to be confirmed in order to be married in the Catholic Church?

The Church has a strong preference that when two Catholics prepare for Marriage, they should be fully initiated into the Catholic Church, which means they have celebrated the Sacraments of Baptism, Confirmation, and Holy Eucharist. The Church teaches that

> Catholics who have not yet received the Sacrament of Confirmation are to receive it to complete their Christian Initiation before they are admitted to Marriage if this can be done without grave inconvenience.[7]

So what exactly does this mean? Well, there may be slight variations in the interpretation of this statement, but, generally speaking and under normal circumstances, any Catholic preparing to

---

7   *The Order for Celebrating Matrimony,* 18.

celebrate the Sacrament of Matrimony who is not confirmed should first participate in a program to prepare first for the Sacrament of Confirmation. Often these programs are just a few weeks in duration but are only offered once or twice a year. This is yet another good reason for getting in touch with the parish as soon as possible once you decide to get married. If there are issues with Confirmation for either party, those issues need to be settled before you can proceed with preparations for the wedding. Your pastor or other member of the parish staff will be able to help you.

There are some instances where it won't be possible to prepare for the Sacrament of Confirmation before Marriage. For example, if the bride or the groom is in the military and is facing deployment in the near future, it might be difficult to compress Marriage preparation and Confirmation preparation into the time available. If the parish does not provide Confirmation preparation every year and such a program is not available in another parish within a reasonable driving distance, the priest or deacon might waive the requirement for Confirmation before the wedding. The expectation, however, is that the person will prepare for and celebrate the Sacrament of Confirmation as soon as possible after the wedding.

14. Do we have to go to confession before we get married?

The Church strongly recommends that you celebrate the Sacrament of Reconciliation as part of the preparation for your wedding, but it is not required. Confession is actually only required in the case of serious sin, although the Church also recommends that all Catholics participate in the Sacrament of Reconciliation at least once a year, whether there is serious sin or not.

Some priests expect that you will go to confession the night of your wedding rehearsal. You may want to inquire about this ahead of time and discuss the possibility of going to confession at another time before your wedding. As mentioned above, the Church does not require that you go to confession before your wedding—unless you have committed a serious sin.

However, even if you do not feel you have committed any serious sins, celebrating the Sacrament of Reconciliation in preparation for your Marriage is a good thing to do. The Sacrament of Reconciliation can help you begin your Marriage with a clean heart and the peace of mind that you have been reconciled with God. Celebrating the Sacrament of Reconciliation can be a gift that you give yourselves as you begin your married life. The Sacrament of Reconciliation also reminds us of the need to forgive and to ask for forgiveness of each other as we go through our married lives.

Your
Catholic Wedding
Ceremony

1. When we contacted our parish to schedule our wedding ceremony, the word "liturgy" was used. What is the liturgy and why is it important?

Liturgy refers to the public worship of the Catholic Church. It is a structured worship service that consists of specific prayers and rituals. For Catholics, there are numerous liturgical celebrations, the most important of which is the celebration of the Eucharist. Most sacramental celebrations take place within the context of a liturgy, whether within Mass or as celebration of a Liturgy of the Word (basically the first part of the Mass in which we hear the Scripture readings proclaimed). Throughout this resource, when you see the word *ceremony* in a religious context, it means *liturgy*.

As baptized Catholics we profess our wedding vows in a public ceremony surrounded by the love and support of our family and friends, our faith community, and the entire communion of saints! The liturgy is a treasure of Roman Catholicism and you are privileged to share in that treasure when you celebrate the Sacrament of Matrimony. And because it is such a treasure, all liturgies celebrated in the Church are bound by certain rules, or liturgical laws. These rules help to preserve the dignity of your wedding ceremony, as a public liturgy of the Church. Our Church is universal, which means that all of our official liturgies are governed by laws of the universal Church and the policies of the Bishops of the United States.

There are Church documents and ritual books that govern the celebration of the seven sacraments of the Church, including Marriage. *The Order of Celebrating Matrimony* is the official book, or ritual book, that your priest or deacon will be using to help prepare for and celebrate your wedding. It includes all the prayers, texts, and rituals for weddings in the Catholic Church in the United States

Because a Catholic wedding is a sacramental celebration, like Baptism or Confirmation, it takes place within or outside of Mass. The Church takes great care to ensure that a wedding is celebrated properly, in conformity to the liturgical practices of the whole Church.

One of the hallmarks of the Catholic liturgy is that it is participative. This means, everyone is invited to sing, pray out loud, sit, stand, and kneel together; to listen to the readings; and to respond to the prayers of the priest. Catholic liturgy is not just the prayer of the priest, or something to watch, it is the prayer of all who are gathered who give praise and thanks to God.

In your role as bride and groom, and "hosts" of your wedding, it is important for you to encourage and enable your guests to be active participants at your wedding liturgy. A good worship aid, as described in question 38, can help with that. You can also be good models of participation when you join in the prayers, the songs, and observe the appropriate postures—standing, sitting, and kneeling—at the appropriate times.

2. Why does the Catholic Church have so many rules about Marriage and the wedding ceremony?

There are two aspects and two answers to this question.

Regarding preparation for Marriage: the Church understands the Sacrament of Matrimony (Marriage) as not only the ceremony in which you are married, but also the life-long relationship that the two of you will maintain for years after the wedding ceremony itself. The Church also believes that Marriage is for life. It is not something into which you enter frivolously or capriciously. Therefore, the Church wants to help you prepare for that life-long relationship in the best way possible so that you and your spouse will be successful in your efforts to live out your Marriage promises, and demonstrate in your relationship a self-sacrificing love for each other and for others that symbolizes the love that Christ has for his Church. Bishops all over the world, and especially the bishops of the United States, have set policies that will encourage and enable you to do so. Those policies include the questionnaires mentioned earlier, along with participation in a pre-Marriage program and careful documentation and record-keeping that you or the priest of a future parish can access.

The liturgy (the official Catholic rituals and ceremonies) is governed by the Catholic Church's liturgical law, most of which is universal (applies to the Church around the world), and some of which is local to particular countries and dioceses. Because the Church is so large, there needs to be consistency in how the liturgy and the sacraments are celebrated. For example, if you went to Mass in another country, you would most likely understand exactly what is happening even though you don't know the language because the basic structure and elements of the liturgy are the same throughout the world. In addition, the Catholic liturgy is highly regulated because it is the public prayer of our Church and it is important that what we say and do at our liturgies truly expresses who we are and what we believe as Catholics. The prayers, the readings, and even the songs we sing are important for what they express in terms of our relationship with and our understanding of God.

When you choose to be married in the Catholic Church, you choose to observe the laws, privileges, and restrictions of a Catholic liturgy. In a sense, you are connected with all those who have gone before you and who will follow you in their pursuit of holiness through the Sacrament of Matrimony. It is a great privilege and an affirmation of your faith to be married in the Catholic Church.

3. Do we both have to be Catholic in order to have a Catholic wedding ceremony?

Only one of you needs to be Catholic in order to be married in the Catholic Church. In fact, whether both of you are Catholic or not will help guide you in your choice of ceremony. The Church provides three options for the wedding ceremony:

- Option 1: Matrimony within Mass
- Option 2: Matrimony without Mass
- Option 3: Matrimony between a Catholic and a Catechumen (a non-Christian preparing to be baptized) or a Non-Christian

If both of you are Catholic, the preferred option is within Mass (option 1), but depending on your particular circumstance and the people who will be present for your celebration, you may decide not to have a Mass (option 2). If one of you was baptized in another Christian faith tradition, there is an assumption that you will use option 2; however, you can also choose the first option if it seems to be a better fit for you and your anticipated guests. If one of you is not baptized (or, if one of you is Jewish, Muslim, or does not have a religious affiliation), the third option is your only choice.

If the person you wish to marry is not Catholic and they would like to be married in their own Christian Church, you must still consult with a Catholic priest or deacon in order to have your Marriage recognized by the Catholic Church. Special permission must be received from the local bishop in order for your Marriage to be considered sacramentally valid in the Catholic Church. Catholic wedding preparation will also be required.

4. Are we required to be married within a Mass?

The celebration of Mass, or the Eucharist, is the most important act in the life of a Christian. It is during Mass that we are shaped by the Word of God, and then receive Christ's very Body and Blood in the mutual sharing of Communion. We are then sent forth into the world, to live as Christian disciples.

Participating in the Eucharist, that is, sharing Communion together as a Church or community, is to share in the very life of Christ himself. The sharing of Communion is a Marriage bond between Christ and the Church. It strengthens us in our relationship with Christ, and with each other. Because the sharing of Communion is the ultimate sign of unity for the Church and other Christian communities do not share the Catholic belief in the Real Presence of Christ in the Eucharist, those who are not Catholic are not permitted to receive Communion.

As a sign of Christ's union with the Church, it is quite fitting—and preferred—that two Catholics celebrate Mass at their wedding.

However, if both of you are Catholic but many or most of your guests are not Catholic, you may want to consider celebrating your wedding at a Liturgy of the Word, without the Eucharist, so that a large number of your guests would not feel uncomfortable or left out at the time of Communion. If this is a concern for both of you, you should discuss this option with your pastor.

If a Catholic is preparing to marry someone who was baptized in another Christian faith tradition, usually, this person will not be permitted to receive Communion. Because of this, the great symbolism of unity that is evident in the sharing of Communion is broken, and so the Church advises that weddings between a Catholic and a person baptized in another Christian faith tradition marry outside of Mass. Although Mass may still be celebrated, this decision should be made very carefully with your parish pastor. Celebrating the Mass when your spouse (and/or guests) cannot receive Communion may create an awkward situation or even offend the spouse who is not Catholic and/or some of your guests. Of course, if the spouse does show faith in the Real Presence of Christ in the Eucharist, they may request special permission from the bishop to be allowed to receive Communion during the wedding Mass. Again, your parish pastor will be able to help you.[1]

If a Catholic is preparing to marry a person who is not baptized, a Mass may not be celebrated.

So, basically, in a Marriage between two Catholics or between a Catholic and a baptized Christian of another denomination, you have the option of having a Mass or not. The decision is best made by the two of you, being sensitive to the beliefs of your guests, the customs and expectations of your families, and your own preferences.

---

1   The United States Bishops have prepared a set of guidelines for receiving Holy Communion in the Catholic Church. These guidelines are often printed in worship aid resources. Some pastors and deacons do require that these guidelines be printed in the worship aid (see question 38) that will be given to guests at your wedding ceremony. You can copy and paste directly from this website: www.usccb.org/prayer-and-worship/the-mass/order -of-mass/liturgy-of-the-eucharist/guidelines-for-the-reception-of -communion.cfm.

5. We are ready to begin preparing our wedding ceremony, but we don't know where to begin! What are the parts of the liturgy?

When it comes to preparing your wedding ceremony, you will not be alone. Your pastor, liturgist, music director, or parish wedding coordinator will gladly help you choose the Scriptures, music, and prayers. Most likely, your parish will require you to meet with one or more of these staff members who will walk you through the Catholic ritual, and they will provide you with the resources you need to prepare a beautiful, meaningful, and sacred ceremony. Your parish music director will need to review with you the places and choices for music. In the meantime, here is an overview of the three different types of ceremonies (liturgies). The following charts detail the elements that make up the three different ceremonies (liturgies). You will also notice which parts you will need to select music for. Your parish music director will help you with musical choices.

Option 1: Matrimony within Mass

Prelude Music

The Introductory Rites
> Entrance Procession and Entrance Song
> Sign of the Cross and Greeting
> Address to the Couple and Assembly
> The Gloria [sung]
> Collect

The Liturgy of the Word
> First Reading [Old Testament; during Easter Time, the Book of Revelation]
> Responsorial Psalm [sung]
> Second Reading [New Testament]
> Gospel Acclamation [sung; no Alleluia during Lent]
> Gospel
> Homily

The Celebration of Matrimony
    Address to the Couple and Witnesses
    Questions before the Consent
    The Consent
    Reception of the Consent
    Sung Acclamation [optional]
    The Blessing and Giving of Rings
    [Blessing and Giving of the *Arras*/Coins]
    Hymn or Canticle [optional]
    The Universal Prayer/Prayer of the Faithful [may be sung]

The Liturgy of the Eucharist
    Preparation of the Altar and Gifts with Offertory Song
      Prayer over the Offerings
      Preface to the Eucharistic Prayer
      Holy, Holy, Holy [sung]
    The Eucharistic Prayer
      Memorial Acclamation [sung]
      Amen [sung]
    The Communion Rite
      Lord's Prayer [may be sung]
      [Blessing and Placing of the *Lazo* or the Veil]
      Nuptial Blessing
      Sign of Peace
      Invitation to Holy Communion
      Distribution of Holy Communion with Communion Song
      Song of Praise [optional]
      Prayer after Communion

The Concluding Rites
    Solemn Blessing
    Dismissal
    Closing Song [optional]

Postlude Music

Option 2: Matrimony without Mass

Prelude Music

The Introductory Rites
    Entrance Procession and Entrance Song
    Sign of the Cross and Greeting
    Address to the Couple and Assembly
    Collect

The Liturgy of the Word
    First Reading [Old Testament; during Easter Time, the Book of Revelation]
    Responsorial Psalm [sung]
    Second Reading [New Testament]
    Gospel Acclamation [sung; no Alleluia during Lent]
    Gospel
    Homily

The Celebration of Matrimony
    Address to the Couple and Witnesses
    Questions before the Consent
    The Consent
    Reception of the Consent
    Sung Acclamation [optional]
    The Blessing and Giving of Rings
    [Blessing and Giving of the *Arras*/Coins]
    Hymn or Canticle [optional]
    The Universal Prayer/Prayer of the Faithful [may be sung]
    Our Father [may be sung]
    [Blessing and Placing of the *Lazo* or the Veil]
    The Nuptial Blessing

The Communion Rite

The following only takes place if, in rare circumstances, Holy Communion is distributed. The Our Father is omitted above and takes place below.

Our Father [may be sung]

Sign of Peace

Invitation to Holy Communion

Distribution of Communion with Song

Prayer after Communion

The Concluding Rites

Simple or Solemn Blessing

Dismissal

Closing Song [optional]

Postlude Music

Option 3: Matrimony between a Catholic and a Catechumen or a Non-Christian

Prelude Music

The Rite of Reception

Greeting of the Couple at the Door

Procession to the Altar

Address to the Couple and Assembly

The Liturgy of the Word

First Reading [Old Testament; during Easter Time, the Book of Revelation]

Responsorial Psalm [sung]

Second Reading [New Testament]

Gospel

Homily

The Celebration of Matrimony
    Address to the Couple and Witnesses
    Questions before the Consent
    The Consent
    Reception of the Consent
    Sung Acclamation [optional]
    The Blessing and Giving of Rings
    [Blessing and Giving of the *Arras*/Coins]
    Hymn or Canticle [optional]
    The Universal Prayer/Prayer of the Faithful [may be sung]
    Our Father [may be sung]
    [Blessing and Placing of the *Lazo* or the Veil]
    Nuptial Blessing

The Concluding Rites
    Simple Blessing
    Concluding Song [optional]

Postlude Music

6. Does our Catholic wedding ceremony have to be inside a church building? Can we have a destination wedding or get married outdoors and still have a Catholic wedding?

The Catholic wedding ceremony should take place in a church building. There is a good reason for this. Your Marriage is a sacrament, and most sacraments are celebrated within a church building, with members of the faith community present to witness the event and provide support and encouragement for those celebrating the sacrament. As a sacrament, the wedding ceremony is a public event in which you and your spouse vow to love and honor each other for the rest of your lives. Your Marriage has an impact not just on the two of you but on everyone around you, and it is the responsibility of your faith community to support you in your commitment to each other.

The church is not just a building. It is the sacred place in which Catholics gather to worship our God, to encounter God in our brothers and sisters in faith, and to celebrate the sacramental moments of our lives. We do this in the presence of Christ in the Blessed Sacrament—the ultimate expression of our faith. All the sacraments take place in the church—your Baptism, your first Communion, your Confirmation, the times you participated in the Sacrament of Reconciliation, every Sunday Mass, and now, your Marriage. Of course you can experience God if you were to marry in another location, however, your Christian Marriage should begin where your life of faith began—the place where you were baptized, the church.

Your love for each other is a symbol of Christ's love for his Church. When you celebrate your Marriage in a church building you are giving credence to that symbolism and to the fact that your Marriage takes place within a particular faith community. While, in reality, many times the only members of a faith community who are present at your wedding may be the presiding priest or deacon and possibly a wedding coordinator or altar server, there is deep symbolism in the fact that you are being married "in the Church." The faith community, the Church, is represented by your family and friends who are present. Celebrating your wedding in the Church offers you a marvelous opportunity to participate more fully in the life of the parish, to attend Mass together as a couple each Sunday, and to raise your children in the faith.

This symbolism is so important that a bishop must give permission for a Catholic Marriage to take place somewhere other than in a church building. Bishops are very reluctant to grant such permissions except in extraordinary circumstances (for example, if a bride or groom is ill or disabled and unable to come to the church). Permission would not be granted to those requesting to be married in a garden, on the beach, or some other place outside of the church.

7. Our parish community is important to us. Can we get married during Sunday Mass?

Your wedding ceremony may take place on most Sundays and, in fact, even most weekdays of the year. Getting married at Sunday Mass is a great way to celebrate your wedding in the midst of the people who should be supporting you in your vocation: the members of your parish.

While a Sunday wedding is not for everyone, those who do get married at this time, do so because of their close ties to the parish, and their desire to have their Marriage witnessed by the members of their faith community as well as by close family and friends. These couples look at the Sunday readings and choose their date based on how closely the readings of the day relate to the celebration of their Marriage. The bride and groom participate in the opening and closing processions of the Mass, and consult with the parish musicians about music that is most appropriate for the readings of the day as well as for the celebration of their Marriage.

Some couples who get married at Sunday Mass host a simple reception afterward for any parishioners who want to join in the celebration and wish them well. Marriage at Sunday Mass is a great witness for the parish community, and helps give everyone a sense of how important their support is for the newly married couple. This is a wonderful option to consider if you are active in your parish or live in a small town where many from the parish are invited to the wedding.

If you would like to be married during Sunday Mass, your parish staff will help you schedule your wedding on an appropriate day. In general, you could do this at any time, but the Church does ask that this not happen on certain days such as Christmas or Easter and on the Sundays during Advent or Lent.

8. The date we have chosen for our Marriage is during Advent/Lent. Will this be a problem?

Generally, getting married during Advent or Lent is not forbidden, although some dioceses and parishes do restrict the practice. Because of the penitential nature of these seasons, the Church recommends that you reconsider getting married during these times. You should be aware that if the parish allows you to get married during Advent or Lent you will need to follow the guidelines for celebrating liturgies during this time. For example, a Lenten environment may already be in place in the sanctuary. You will most likely have to agree that you will not move what is already in place. The music and environment should also be scaled back (you may not even be allowed to have flowers). Your parish pastor, liturgist, music director, or wedding coordinator will be able to help you. When setting your date with the parish, it's a good idea to ask about the liturgical season in which you are getting married, and what the church will look like on that particular day.

9. Who presides (or officiates) at a Catholic wedding? May a deacon preside? May a Protestant minister preside since one of us attends a Protestant Church?

A priest or deacon must officiate (or preside) at a Catholic wedding ceremony. A priest always officiates (presides) if a Mass takes place. A deacon may be present during the Mass; however, he may not witness the vows (exchange of consent) at Mass unless he first receives special permission from the bishop. Usually, this happens if the deacon has a special relationship with the bride or groom (perhaps a parent or uncle). If a deacon is present during Mass, he may hold the *Book of the Gospels* during the entrance procession, proclaim the Gospel, give the homily, and/or read the petitions during the Universal Prayer (Prayer of the Faithful). If the wedding takes place without Mass, a deacon may always preside (this includes the witnessing of the vows, or exchange of consent).

If the bride or groom has a relationship with the minister of another Christian tradition, and wants that minister to be part of the ceremony, the minister may assist with permission from the Catholic pastor. The Protestant minister may join in the procession, or be present in the sanctuary. You might also ask him or her to proclaim one of the readings or give a reflection. However, the Catholic priest or deacon must receive your vows (that is, witness the exchange of consent) in the name of the Church. Special permission may also be granted for a religious leader from another faith (such as a Jewish rabbi) to participate in some way. Some dioceses may have different practices, and so it is best to approach this issue with your Catholic pastor well in advance of your wedding.

In some areas of the country, where there may be a serious lack of priests and deacons, the bishop can delegate a layperson (a person who is not ordained but is Catholic) to assist at Marriages. This person would be selected and prepared by the Church to work with the couple in preparing for their Marriage as well as perform the wedding ceremony. The designated person would witness and receive your vows in the name of the Church.

10. Are there any restrictions on what the bride, groom, or members of the wedding party may wear?

Your parish may have a dress code for members of the wedding party. Because you are choosing to get married in a Catholic church there needs to be some sense of decorum and modesty for such a ceremony. You—the bride and groom—will be standing in front of the priest or deacon as you profess your vows, and you may be climbing steps into the church sanctuary at the beginning of, or at some point during, the ceremony. You are participating in a religious ceremony that celebrates the sacrament of your Marriage. Extremely low-cut or revealing dresses on the bride or any of her bridesmaids are inappropriate. Likewise, think about how the bride and her bridesmaids will be able to process and move about.

You may also want to caution those you have chosen to read the Scriptures or assist with the distribution of Communion about wearing dresses that are very short or inappropriately revealing, especially if they will be entering the sanctuary to read or to help with the distribution of Communion. Perhaps the parish has a dress code for liturgical ministers that you may consult for guidance as to what is appropriate.

11. Is there a limit to the number of bridesmaids and groomsmen we can have?

It may be surprising to some couples that the Catholic wedding ceremony doesn't include or require bridesmaids or groomsmen. Instead, the Church simply requires that you have two witnesses (of the same or different gender), that is, two people who can attest to having been present at your wedding and witnessed the ceremony taking place. The witnesses' names are recorded in the parish records and they may be required to sign the marriage license that will be submitted to the state. Although it's preferred that your witnesses are Catholic, this is not a requirement. Whether or not you have any other attendants is entirely up to you. The roles customarily known as the maid (or matron) of honor and the best man, in practice, usually fill the role of witnesses.

In ancient times, many witnesses were required, which is how the tradition of having many attendants developed. Today, the number of bridesmaids and groomsmen is often determined by the formality of your wedding ceremony. Sometimes it is determined by the number of friends or relatives a bride and groom would like to include in their wedding. If you are planning to have a large number of attendants you might want to discuss this early on with the presiding priest or deacon. Some parishes may have limitations on the number of attendants—often due to space constraints. If you are getting married in a small church, a large number of attendants might make the space appear cramped. Think about the space in which your wedding will take place along with all the other considerations about inviting close family members and friends to be in your wedding party. The additional members of your wedding party also do not have to be Catholic.

12. What processional options are there for the bridal party? According to our pastor, it is the Church's preference for the couple to walk down the aisle together. We thought the father walked the bride down the aisle. Why is the Church's preference different than every wedding we've ever been to or seen on television?

Although it is an age-old custom for the bride's father to walk her down the aisle and "give her away," it is a surprise to many that this custom is actually not part of the Catholic wedding ceremony. The Church provides two options for the entrance procession:

Option 1:
At the appointed time, the Priest . . . goes with the servers to the door of the church, receives the bridal party, and warmly greets them, showing that that the Church shares in their joy.

The procession to the altar then takes place in the customary manner.[2]

Option 2
At the appointed time, the Priest, . . . goes with servers to the place prepared for the couple or to his chair.

When the couple have arrived at their place, the Priest receives them and warmly greets them, showing that the Church shares in their joy.[3]

Notice in both of these options that there is no mention of the father walking his daughter down the aisle, nor is there mention of bridesmaids, or even flower girls and ring bearers. There is no mention of the groom, accompanied by groomsmen, waiting in the front for his

---

2   *The Order of Celebrating Matrimony*, 45, 46.
3   *The Order of Celebrating Matrimony*, 48, 49.

bride to enter. Instead, in both options presented above, it is "the couple" who walk in together.

The first option presumes that the bride and groom will be included in the procession. The priest receives the "bridal party" at the door of the church. This presumes the presence of the couple and their two witnesses. When the Church talks about the procession occurring in a "customary manner," she is referring to a "liturgical procession," rather than a procession of dignitaries or attendants to a princess or queen. A liturgical procession is a procession of liturgical ministers: those who will take part in the ceremony.

In Catholic liturgy, everything that is done has a greater, symbolic meaning. Our prayers, gestures, and movements always point to a bigger reality—they express what we believe. A liturgical procession symbolizes our journey to Christ. Those who take part in the procession walk through the gathered faithful, the Body of Christ, and reach their final destination, the altar which represents the sacrifice of Christ. As baptized Christians, we journey through our life with one purpose—to change, grow, and mature to be more like Christ, to be in greater relationship with Christ. This is what the liturgical procession symbolizes. At a wedding, the procession of the liturgical minister, the witnesses, and finally, the bride and groom, reflect the journey that these two people are making together—to live their lives as a married couple sharing in the love of Christ.

The liturgical procession begins with the cross-bearer, who may be accompanied by servers carrying candles and/or incense. Other liturgical ministers, such as the readers, follow and the principle minister, who is usually the priest (but also may be a deacon), comes at the end of the procession.

This does not mean that you may not have bridesmaids, groomsmen, a flower girl, or ring bearer. If a couple has additional attendances, they will follow the officiant and precede the couple. At a wedding, however, the priest or deacon is the official witness of the Catholic Church, and the bride and groom are the principle ministers of the sacrament. This means they are the last ones to walk into the church in the opening procession. The Church teaches and believes that husbands and wives are equal partners in Marriage, and the rituals associated with the Sacrament of Matrimony affirm that belief. A couple walking at the start of their Marriage ceremony speaks loudly that this is a partnership of two equals, both consenting to the Marriage.

If it is important to the bride for her father to walk her down the aisle, a good compromise is to have the groom accompanied by his parents followed by the bride accompanied by her parents. They would still be preceded by the liturgical ministers, and the members of the wedding party.

The second option for the opening procession presents a simpler option that may be adapted. If this is chosen, the priest and ministers (servers) are not required to process down the main aisle, although this is certainly an option. They can simply take their places and wait for the couple to arrive at the place that was prepared for them. However, again, the option does expect that "the couple" process to the place where they will be greeted by the priest or deacon. There is no mention that the couple is escorted by their witnesses or parents, although, there is no reason that they could not be included. What is important here is the focus on the couple, which, as noted above, symbolizes the journey they are making together.

Of course, weddings are one aspect of life in which traditions play an important role, and old customs and practices are sometimes difficult to change. The origins of a father walking his daughter down the aisle are from the days of arranged Marriages when a daughter was considered the property of her father. The father gave his daughter to her new husband along with a dowry of money and/ or other household items. Even though today's brides do not have parents who consider them to be their property, some still like to maintain the custom of the father walking his daughter down the aisle. This custom is not forbidden by the Church, and most officiating priests and deacons will allow you to follow this custom if you feel strongly about it. Unlike what we often see on TV or the internet, the Church chooses to place emphasis on the partnership of the couple. In the wedding ceremony, you "freely give [your]selves to each other and accept each other."[4]

I suggest you talk seriously about this together and then have a discussion with the priest or deacon who will be officiating at your wedding. The second form mentioned above does provide room for adapting your procession. Let me give you a few examples from my own experience:

At our daughter's wedding, she and her husband chose to have the members of the wedding party process in first, followed by the groom (accompanied by his parents), and then the bride (accompanied by her parents).

At our son's wedding, the bride really wanted her father to walk her down the aisle, and the groom wanted his parents to accompany him down the aisle. The procession was led by the priest (there were no altar servers in this small church wedding), followed by members of the bridal party, then the groom with his parents, followed by the bride's mother and brother, and finally the bride with her father. (Our son was married in a small church and the aisle was not wide enough for the three of us to walk together, so his father and I walked slightly behind him.)

Almost forty years ago, my sister was married in a Lutheran church a few years after my own wedding. She and her husband-to-be greeted everyone as they arrived, then walked together down the aisle in the opening procession, behind the minister, their two witnesses (bridal party), and parents of both the bride and groom. I remember wishing someone had told me about that a few years earlier when my husband and I were married because I loved the symbolism of the couple walking together to the altar!

At a Sunday Mass, the bride and groom walked in the regular opening procession, behind the altar servers and in front of the deacon and priest. Since it was a regular Sunday Mass, the priest came at the end of the procession.

---

4   *The Order of Celebrating Matrimony*, 2.

An additional option is to have the members of the bridal party followed by the parents of both the groom and the bride, followed by the couple.

So depending on what symbolism and traditions are important to you, and also depending on the customs in the parish and even the floor plan of the church, you have numerous options.

Don't leave this discussion until the night of the rehearsal! It may also eliminate a lot of tension if the people in your wedding party are informed of the preparations before the last minute.

13. We would like our niece to be the flower girl but she's only a year old and is not able to walk. How do we get her down the aisle? We have seen other couples use a red wagon. Can we do this?

You might want to reconsider that question. Let me give you an example. I have a two-year-old grandson who is adorable and very well-loved by all our family, but I would never expect him to "perform" in a wedding. Young children can be very unpredictable, especially in unfamiliar situations. They also don't understand the significance of the event and the important role they are being asked to carry out. When looking at the options available for your Catholic wedding, you want to make choices that will help people pray, and that will help people enter into the sacredness of this event. By choosing very young children to participate in the wedding procession, you are opening yourself up to the possibility that the child will disrupt the ceremony and possibly create a scene or unnecessary tension by refusing to participate, or there could be some type of mishap on the way down the aisle.

A very young child should be with his or her mother or father during the ceremony and not expected to be a part of the wedding party—not even if pulled down the aisle in a wagon.

If your sister expects you to include her young child in your wedding, perhaps you can find something for them to do at the reception.

Keep in mind that whatever you do, and whomever you choose, your wedding ceremony should contribute to the prayerfulness of everyone gathered. A Catholic wedding is a religious ritual, a sacramental experience, in which you promise to love and be faithful to each other for the rest of your lives. It is not a showcase for your young nieces and/or nephews, no matter how adorable they are.

14. We recently attended our friend's wedding. They love animals just as we do, and their dog was the ring-bearer. It was so cute. Can we have a dog in the wedding party?

Pets are very important companions for some of us, and an important part of our lives. However, even more so than young children, animals should not be included among the attendants at your wedding. The purpose of your wedding party is to witness your Marriage and to support and stand by you on this important sacramental occasion.

When you include a dog or other animal in the ceremony, you are making a spectacle of the animal. Your pet may be upset or spooked by the large number of people, or by being in a situation or place with which they are not familiar. As a result, their behavior will most likely not be what you expect or hope for. You also run the risk of offending someone, or having an adverse effect on someone who has pet allergies or who is afraid of dogs (or cats, or whatever animal you are considering).

Please don't consider including pets in your wedding party. Animals are not able to participate in the prayer of the assembly, and you will be creating a very stressful situation for your pet and possibly for others participating in your wedding.

15. Where will we be seated in the church during the ceremony? Are there special seating arrangements for us? Our wedding party? Our guests?

The place where you sit during the wedding ceremony will depend a good deal on the layout of the church along with the preference of the priest or deacon officiating (presiding). This is a good question to ask fairly early on in your wedding preparations so that there are no misunderstandings at the rehearsal or on the day of the wedding.

Many priests like to have the couple sit in the sanctuary, either next to the priest or to one side. This is to make it clear to everyone that the bride and groom are the ministers in a wedding. The priest or deacon is the official Church witness to your wedding, but you and your spouse are the actual ministers during this ceremony. You minister to each other as you speak your vows and exchange wedding rings.

Some parishes have the couple seated in the front pew, or in chairs placed in front of the first pew. Doing so encourages the attention of the assembly to be directed on the proclamation of the Word and the celebration of the Eucharist rather than toward the couple. It is a matter of hospitality that you sit in view of everyone in the church, and especially that you stand for your vows and exchange of rings in a place where you can be easily seen and heard by your guests.

The wedding party usually sits at the front of the church—perhaps in the front pew or in the pew directly behind the bride and groom. Again, this is something that is a matter of parish policy, based on the architecture of the building, on the preferences of the presider, and on the preferences of the bride and groom.

As far as the seating of your wedding guests, there is a tradition of seating guests on the "bride's side" or the "groom's side," but this is not a requirement, nor is it even encouraged. It is much more hospitable and conducive to a fuller and more participative celebration if people are seated on either side as they arrive. You may want to have special areas for your close family, but otherwise consider having your ushers invite people to sit wherever they want. Just be sure to communicate your wishes to those who will be serving as ushers. Please ask your ushers (or other hospitality ministers) to fill up the pews in the front of the Church first, leaving the back pews for latecomers.

16. Many of our family and friends are not Catholic. We would like them to be involved in our wedding ceremony. May someone who isn't Catholic serve as reader or in one of the other roles?

The various liturgies or ceremonies of the Church require the assistance of liturgical ministers who fill such roles as reading the passages from Scripture, assisting the priest or deacon (altar servers), distributing Communion (extraordinary ministers of Holy Communion), leading the music (cantor), and greeting guests as they arrive (ushers, greeters, hospitality ministers). It is preferred that you have Catholics serve as liturgical ministers at your wedding. Consider choosing friends and relatives who already have experience in carrying out the particular ministries of reader, cantor, extraordinary minister of Holy Communion, and altar server. Ideally, altar servers are from the parish in which you are getting married. They are familiar with the customary way of serving at the parish; they know where to stand, how the procession moves, and where to place things such as the chalice and altar linens; and they are comfortable serving in a space with which they are familiar, and they know the expectations of the parish priest(s).

Extraordinary ministers of Holy Communion—those who help the priests and deacons distribute Communion to those present—must be Catholic. If you have guests who are extraordinary ministers in the parish in which you are getting married, consider them first to carry out this ministry. Alternatively, if you have guests who serve as extraordinary ministers in parishes other than the one where you are getting married, talk with the priest about inviting them to serve and arrange for a time for them to practice and walk through the procedures. The presiding priest or the parish liturgy director may need to verify that the persons you are inviting to serve are in good standing at their own parish, so don't wait until the last minute to work this out.

It is also permissible for a priest to "commission" a person for one-time service as an extraordinary minister. This means that the priest can give special permission for someone who is not an extraordinary minister to serve in that capacity on a one-time basis for a particular occasion, such as a wedding or funeral.

Some parishes provide readers for weddings. If you have a guest who is a reader either in the church in which you are getting married or in their own parish they would be a good candidate to serve as a reader at your wedding. Some priests will also permit a baptized person who is not Catholic to assist with the readings if it is someone who has the skill to do so. If you would like your cousin, who is not Catholic, to proclaim one of the readings, it is best to first consult with your pastor.

Ushers (and greeters or hospitality ministers, if you choose to use them) can be male or female and do not need to be Catholic to serve at your wedding. Ushers are responsible for helping people find their seats in the church and are considered ministers of hospitality for parish liturgies. Your groomsmen can serve as ushers at your wedding or you can have others, even regular parish ushers, assist with seating people for the liturgy. Greeters, who are also liturgical ministers of hospitality, do just that: greet people as they come into the church. It is possible, and not uncommon, for the ushers at a wedding to also greet people as they arrive. There are a number of ways this can be done, depending on the number of people you choose to have in your wedding party, the number of guests you are expecting, the configuration of the church, etc. Ushers at your wedding do not need to be Catholic, although it is best to be specific about what you want them to do. A little instruction can go a long way toward resolving awkward circumstances. For instance, at my son's wedding, the gentlemen who were asked to be ushers decided to greet everyone while my very pregnant daughter led people to their seats! You might also consider greeting your guests yourselves.

Cantors also need to be familiar with Catholic rituals so that they can help the liturgy flow smoothly and be comfortable with the cues for singing at various times, particularly when your wedding is celebrated within Mass.

Before considering who you will ask to serve in the various liturgical ministries at your wedding, remember that those people should be chosen for their skill or qualifications rather than just because of their significance to you. If you want a bridesmaid to read at your wedding, and she is somewhat shy or has no experience using a microphone or speaking in front of a group of people, you risk the possibility that the reading will be done poorly and/or your guests will not hear or understand the Scripture passage you so carefully chose. Also, whomever you invite to read the Scriptures at your wedding should be given ample time to prepare. They should be given a copy of the reading at least a week in advance for that very purpose. Of course, at the wedding it would be expected that they read from the Lectionary (the book of Scripture readings for Masses in the Catholic Church) or, in some cases, from a special binder prepared by the priest or wedding coordinator. Separate sheets of paper should never be used. Readers should be present at the wedding rehearsal so that they can familiarize themselves with the placement of the ambo (the special lectern where the Scripture readings are proclaimed), the microphone, and may practice proclaiming the readings.

It is best and most appropriate that someone who is Catholic and who will be receiving Communion bring up the gifts of bread and wine if Mass is celebrated. The bread and wine will be transformed into the Body and Blood of Christ. It would not be hospitable to ask someone to present the gifts of bread and wine if they themselves are not invited to come forward to receive Communion. Some couples choose to bring the gifts forward themselves, which is a perfectly lovely and acceptable thing to do.

17. Why does the Church insist on having Scripture readings? Why can't we use a beautiful poem instead?

If you have a beautiful poem you would like read on your wedding day, the best place to do so is at the reception, perhaps immediately before you cut the cake, or as part of the prayer before everyone eats. If you are having a rehearsal dinner, that would also be an appropriate time and place, or perhaps you can have the poem printed in a worship aid provided for all your guests.[5] This could be printed on the last page or on the back cover of the worship aid.

Only readings from Scripture are allowed at a Catholic wedding. In fact, every Catholic ritual includes readings from the Scriptures. This part of the ritual is called the Liturgy of the Word. The purpose of the Liturgy of the Word (whether celebrated within or outside Mass) is to give everyone the opportunity to hear God speaking to us in the readings from Sacred Scripture. God's Word is important to us, not just as something that was written thousands of years ago, but as a message that has relevance for us today. The Scripture readings have been chosen by the Church to bring us God's Word and to help us grow closer to God. The homily (formerly called a sermon) illuminates God's Word for us and helps us relate to the Word today. The reading and hearing of God's Word is so important that no other type of reading is permitted at Mass or at any service that includes a Liturgy of the Word. The Church teaches that:

> When the Sacred Scriptures are read in the Church, God himself speaks to his people, and Christ, present in his word, proclaims the Gospel. Therefore, the readings from the Word of God are to be listened to reverently by everyone, for they are an element of the greatest importance in the Liturgy.[6]

It's been already mentioned in this resource, that anything done at your wedding should be focused around the prayer of the gathered assembly and the sacredness of the moment. This would certainly be

---

5 See page 20.
6 *General Instruction of the Roman Missal*, 29.

accomplished through the use of Sacred Scripture at your wedding. What is amazing about the Scriptures is that, even though they were written thousands of years ago, there is still so much that speaks to us today. Take a look at the suggested readings for your Catholic wedding and you will see that in each of them there is a message that can be applied to our lives today.

Your wedding ceremony in the Catholic Church is a celebration of your love for each other within the context of God's love for all of us. This love can be beautifully expressed in the readings, especially if you are careful about whom you choose to proclaim those readings. Hopefully you have the choice of someone who has a love of Scripture and who is skilled at conveying God's message to everyone present.

18. Where do we find the readings to choose for our wedding?

Liturgy Training Publications (the publisher of the book you are holding in your hands right now) has published a wonderful booklet that contains all the suggested Scripture readings for weddings, along with commentaries on the readings and suggestions for readings that work well together for your wedding ceremony. It is called *United in Christ: Preparing the Liturgy of the Word at Catholic Weddings* and can be purchased through the LTP website (www.ltp.org) or from other retailers that sell Catholic books. The readings, along with many other resources for preparing your Catholic wedding, can also be found at www.foryourMarriage.org. This site is sponsored by the United States Conference of Catholic Bishops and has reliable information for anyone getting married in the Catholic Church, including a very well done video about the Marriage ritual that explains the choices of rites and other options within those rites. There are some good questions at the end of the video. Your parish will also be able to help you select the readings.

My recommendation to couples is that you look at all the readings for wedding ceremonies in the Catholic Church during a period of time. Spend some time reflecting on each reading (no more than two or three readings at one sitting), and talk together about what each reading means to you and whether or not it is relevant enough to be included in your wedding ceremony. Generally you will choose one reading from the Old Testament, one reading from the New Testament, and a Gospel. Some priests and deacons prefer to choose the Gospel themselves, while allowing the couple to choose the first two readings. Discuss your choices with the priest or deacon who will be officiating, and ask if you will be choosing the Gospel or if he prefers to choose the Gospel himself. You will also need to choose a Responsorial Psalm, which is usually done in consultation with the musician. There are different musical settings for the psalms so your musician will perhaps play them for you or provide a CD or a link to a website with a number of options.

19. Do we have to pick the prayers for the wedding ceremony? We are confused as to where to find them and how to know what to select. Is this something we should be concerned with, or can our pastor or parish staff do this for us?

Generally speaking, you do not need to be concerned about selecting the various prayers used at your wedding celebration. The Church encourages couples to select the Scripture readings, the music, the form for the exchange of consent (the vows), blessing of rings, Universal Prayer (Prayer of the Faithful), and the Nuptial Blessing. If you will be married during a Mass, there are additional prayers that need to be chosen. Some priests or deacons may wish to work with you in choosing the various prayers, but many would rather choose the prayers themselves. It's really a decision between you and the priest or deacon who will be officiating (presiding) at your wedding as to how involved you will be in choosing the prayers. In my parish, our pastor prefers to choose the prayers himself, but if a couple has a strong preference for particular prayers, he will usually accommodate their wishes. Your parish should provide you with resources that will help you to select texts from the options the Church provides for your ceremony.

20. Our pastor recommended that we write our own Prayer of the Faithful. We're not sure what this prayer is or how to write it. Do you have recommendations for how to do this?

One prayer you can definitely "customize" is the Prayer of the Faithful (or Universal Prayer): the intercessions that take place immediately after the actual Celebration of Matrimony. This prayer is actually part of our response to the Word of God we have heard in the Scriptures, as well as an opportunity for us to name specific concerns and intentions. The names of your loved ones who have died can be included in this prayer.

The Church gives us guidelines for the Universal Prayer because in this prayer we join with other Catholics all over the world in praying for various intentions. There is a recommended structure to the prayer that moves from world-wide concerns and issues to the specific intentions of the local community.

The series of intentions is usually:

1. For the needs of the universal Church;
2. For public authorities and the people of the world;
3. For those burdened by any difficulty (such as victims of wars or natural disasters);
4. For the local community (this includes the two of you, your family, deceased loved ones and other specific intentions you may wish to include).

There are a variety of resources available to help you when choosing or composing the intercessions for your wedding. The parish may have a set of intercessions they generally use, and the priest, deacon, or liturgist can guide you to various resources and/or give you sample intercessions if you wish to write your own. Just remember to keep each intercession brief, follow the format generally used in the parish, and do not have an excessive number of intercessions. Listen to the intercessions read at weekend Masses at your parish to get an idea of format, length, and number of intercessions for your wedding.

Your parish may also have petitions that have already been written. You might consider reviewing these options and decide if you would like to use them at your own wedding.

21. Do we have to kneel during the ceremony?

If you are celebrating your Marriage without a Mass, there is no occasion to kneel during the ceremony, except possibly for the Nuptial Blessing near the end. You will stand for the beginning of the service; sit during the Liturgy of the Word; and stand for the exchange of vows and rings, and the intercessions; and stand or kneel for the final blessing.

If you are celebrating your Marriage within a Mass, you and everyone else in the church should observe the usual postures during Mass. The only time you should be doing something different from the rest of the assembly is when you are exchanging your vows and rings, and when you are receiving the Nuptial Blessing. At those times, you will be standing (or kneeling for the blessing) and probably everyone else will be seated.

If you have concerns about this, I suggest that you ask the questions well before the rehearsal to avoid any last-minute tension. Some pastors or parishes may have customs that differ from the norm and you would want to have an opportunity to discuss them ahead of time.

22. May we write our own vows?

Couples often wish to write their own vows as a personal expression of their love and commitment to each other. You have probably witnessed this at other weddings you have attended. A personal expression of love can most certainly be included in your program or worship aid or said at your reception dinner, perhaps at the wedding toast or before the cutting of the cake.

However, in the Catholic wedding ceremony, couples may not write their own vows. The term *vow* is actually not used in the Catholic ceremony. Instead, the vows are called the *exchange of consent* and it is one of the most important parts of the wedding ceremony—so important, that the Church provides the text that you are to use. No other words may be said other than the options the Church provides.

The exchange of consent is important because it acknowledges that the couple has come to be married by their own free will, that they have not been forced or coerced in any way, that they are prepared to enter into the covenant of Marriage and love each other for life, and that they are open to life. The exchange of consent is received by the priest or deacon and it verifies the covenant before God and in the presence of the Church (those present at the wedding ceremony). It is the exchange of consent in the presence of the Church's witnesses that establishes the validity of the sacramental nature of Marriage.[7] There are two options for the exchange of consent. Your pastor or parish staff contact will help you decide from among the options.

23. Why are we not permitted to drink alcohol before the wedding ceremony?

Catholic parishes have strict rules about drinking alcohol before the wedding ceremony. Of course, this is a practical reason, as alcohol can unnecessarily cause disturbances and embarrass those involved. However, refraining from drinking alcohol until after the ceremony has important implications for the sacramental nature of the Marriage. As explained in question 22, the exchange of consent is one of the most important parts of the Catholic ceremony. Because the couple declares before God in the presence of the Catholic community that they are freely seeking to enter into the covenant or Sacrament of Matrimony, they must do so in an unaltered condition. Alcohol inhibits one from responding with full capacity and intention; therefore, they are unable to freely give consent. If a person is unable to give consent, the sacrament cannot be celebrated. If it is suspected that any member of the wedding party is under the influence, the wedding ceremony must be cancelled immediately.

---

7   See also page 6.

24. We didn't realize that the Unity Candle was not part of the Catholic Church's wedding ceremony. We would still like to add this to the ceremony. What are our options?

The Unity Candle is not part of the Catholic wedding ceremony. It is a custom of fairly recent origin, which makes more sense to observe if the couple is getting married outside of the Catholic Church in a ceremony that has little religious ritual and/or symbolism. The Catholic wedding ceremony is already rich in symbolism and there is no need to include additional elements. The exception for adding elements to the ceremony is for some customs or rituals that are particular to various cultures, and which have been used for generations. When you celebrate your Marriage within the Mass, you are already participating in the highest form of love and unity there is: the Eucharist! In the Eucharistic Prayer of the Mass, the priest prays that all may be one and that all may be transformed into the Body of Christ. When the newly married couple shares in the reception of the Eucharist, they are celebrating their unity with each other and with everyone present as members of the Body of Christ. Even at a Liturgy of the Word celebration (without a Mass) there is ample emphasis on the love of the bride and groom for each other as a sign of the love Christ has for his Church.

Consider these symbols and rituals of the wedding ceremony: the way the opening procession is carried out; the exchange of vows in the same words that have been used by thousands of Catholic couples over many years; the ritual exchange of rings and the accompanying words; the Nuptial Blessing which calls down God's blessing on the bride and the groom; the Prayer of the Faithful, which can include prayers for various family members both living and deceased, as well as a prayer for all married couples and for those preparing for Marriage.

The exchange of wedding rings, the Nuptial Blessing, and most other prayers used in the wedding ceremony all contribute to the understanding and symbolism of unity for the couple getting married. When the priest or deacon receives your vows, he says, "What

God joins together, let no one put asunder."[8] When you place the wedding ring on your new spouse's finger, you do so "as a sign of [your] love and fidelity."[9] The beautiful Nuptial Blessing makes numerous references to the love and unity between a husband and wife.

In addition, candles are already a part of the environment for any liturgical celebration in a Catholic church, and it would be more appropriate to light the Paschal candle for your wedding ceremony. The Paschal candle is the large, stately candle that is blessed and lit at every Easter Vigil (the most important Catholic liturgy of the year) to represent Christ as the Light of the World and to remind us of our Baptism into Christ. It is a beautiful representation of Christ and the unity you share with each other and with the rest of the Body of Christ, the light of the world. It is a powerful and strong symbol of the presence of Christ in your Marriage.

To be sure, the Unity Candle can be a touchy subject in some parishes and dioceses. There are priests and bishops who forbid it, and some who will allow it even though it is not Catholic ritual and not included in the Church's ritual for Marriage. Don't be surprised if your parish does not permit the use of the Unity Candle. Many priests are opposed to it (mostly because it is an unnecessary addition to the ceremony and one that is not as strong or powerful as the symbols mentioned above). For some parishes, it may even be a practical issue: in my own parish because of the air conditioning in the church, all the ritual candles have glass followers, or "chimneys" which protect the flames and prevent the wax from dripping. Candles placed in or near the sanctuary without followers melt and burn so unevenly that they make a huge mess!

If the Unity Candle is not permitted in your parish, and you really want to include it on your wedding day, perhaps you can have one at the reception, on the table with the wedding cake or at the table where you and your new spouse will be eating. Make it part of

---

8   *The Order of Celebrating Matrimony,* 64.
9   *The Order of Celebrating Matrimony,* 67.

the prayer before everyone eats, or use it at some other time during the reception.

25. We found a great idea on Pinterest where different colors of sand are poured into a vase to symbolize the joining of two people as one. Why isn't this allowed in the Catholic Church?

I think the question to ask here is why would you want to include this ritual at your wedding? What significance does it have for you and your intended spouse?

The Catholic wedding ceremony is rich with symbolism. If you are married during Mass, you have the Eucharist as the primary symbol of love and unity. The readings you choose are also full of rich imagery. The exchange of vows and the exchange of rings form the core of the wedding ceremony. The Sign of Peace at Mass signifies the unity, reconciliation, and peace of all present before sharing in the Body and Blood of Christ. Your words of commitment and the gestures you use speak volumes. There is really no need for additional rituals or secular images.

Again, if this particular idea of expression appeals to you, find a way to incorporate it at your reception, not your ceremony.

26. We would like to honor a family member who has passed away. How can we do this at our wedding ceremony?

Many couples like to include the name of deceased parents, grandparents, or other close relatives in the Prayer of the Faithful, which is a part of all Catholic wedding liturgies.[10] A special petition can be included with their names. It is also possible that the priest or deacon officiating at your Marriage could mention your father (or other recently deceased close relative) in his homily if you discuss it with him ahead of time. Some couples wear an item of clothing, or a special keepsake that previously belonged to their deceased relative.

---

10 See also page 48.

27. As a couple, how can we address the needs of the poor at our wedding?

As Catholics, the needs of the poor should never be far from our mind. As you make preparations for your wedding, perhaps you can reach out and offer some help to those in your community and throughout the world who are most in need.

The Church tells us we must take care of the poor at all times. On your wedding day, you can honor this mandate by doing something in support of those who have little or nothing.

Here are a couple of suggestions for incorporating the needs of the poor into your wedding:

- One of your gift registries could be for a charitable organization. For example, you might consider requesting that guests donate to Heifer International, an organization that uses donations to provide animals to people in third world countries to help them become self-sufficient.

- You may fill baskets with food and supplies for the parish food pantry and choose people to bring it forward along with the gifts of bread and wine.

- Include a petition for the poor and the oppressed in the Universal Prayer (or Prayer of the Faithful).[11]

- With permission from the parish staff, donate your flowers for the parish to use to decorate the church or parish offices or take as gifts for the sick and homebound.

- In lieu of party favors at the reception, consider making a donation to your favorite charity (human or animal) on behalf of your guests.

- After the wedding, consider donating the wedding gown to a charity. There are organizations that will sell the gown to raise funds for breast cancer needs, and others who donate to the poor or even use the gown to make burial garments for deceased infants. (The dress could even be used to make your own child's baptismal garment or first Communion dress.)

---

11 See page 48.

As you think about the needs of the poor, consider these questions: Does your parish collect food for the poor? Does the parish regularly support any local charities? Do you have a favorite charitable cause? Your wedding ceremony celebrates your love for each other, which mirrors the love of Christ for his Church, which includes the poor. Consider ways you can share your wealth and your mutual love with those who are less fortunate than you.

28. May we give our mothers, or both our parents flowers at the Sign of Peace?

There is nothing in the Catholic wedding ceremony that mentions the giving of flowers at this time (or at any other time during the ceremony), but if it is something you wish to do at your wedding, I suggest you talk with the officiating priest or deacon. This practice may be discouraged in most parishes simply because there is already so much symbolism in the ceremony itself that there is no need to add additional symbols. You might want to give flowers to your parents at another time—perhaps before or after the ceremony—but, if this is important to you and you have a solid reason for wanting to do so, bring it up in your discussion with the priest, deacon, liturgist, or wedding coordinator. Giving flowers to the mothers during the Mass is a duplication of symbols, since you have already provided them with flowers before Mass.

29. We are from another country and now live in the United States. Our home country has certain wedding traditions or rituals. In what ways can our wedding reflect our cultural heritage?

The Church's wedding ceremony allows for some cultural customs to be incorporated into the ceremony as long as they are not connected with superstition or they do not contradict our Catholic faith in any way.

If you wish to include any customs particular to your culture that your family has observed over the years, please be sure to discuss these with the presiding priest or deacon. For example, it is a Hispanic custom (approved for use in the United States) for the wedding ceremony to include an exchange of coins (*arras*) after the giving of rings and/or the placing of the veil (*lazo*) before the Nuptial Blessing. These customs each have a specific meaning, which is in harmony with the Catholic understanding of Marriage. The coins represent the expression of commitment between the couple to share what they are and what they have, to administer responsibly the temporal goods of their Marriage, and to overcome egoism. The *lazo* or veil is placed over the couple to symbolize their coming together in mutual agreement, and the recognition of their total acceptance of each other with self-giving love.

Any customs that have been part of your family's tradition should be discussed with the priest or deacon presiding at your wedding fairly early during the preparation stages so that there will be sufficient preparation and understanding among everyone involved.

30. May we place flowers before a statue or image of the Blessed Virgin Mary?

In the United States, a tradition has emerged where the bride, either by herself, or accompanied by her new spouse, places flowers before a statue or an image of the Blessed Virgin Mary and remains there in prayer while the "Ave Maria," or another Marian hymn, is sung. This often takes place after Communion. Some may be surprised that this tradition is actually not part of the Catholic wedding ceremony. As noted elsewhere, the wedding ceremony is a sacramental rite of the Church. As a sacramental rite, it involves the *public worship* of the gathered community. Marian devotions, such as praying before a statue or an image of Mary, are a form of personal prayer that does not belong within the wedding ceremony. The Marriage rite is powerful and the symbols of unity that are conveyed within the ceremony stand on their own. When we begin to add extra layers to them, like the Unity Candle or devotion to Mary, we end up confusing the focus and diluting the strength of the ritual itself. Simply put, sometimes we have to remember that "less is more." Trust the power of the rite. The giving of consent, the exchange of rings, the language of the Nuptial Blessing, the sharing of Communion (if Mass is celebrated), and the love of the couple are—and should be—the primary focus of the ritual.

For couples who have a special devotion to Mary, and would like to incorporate this devotion in their ceremony, there is a more appropriate time for this to happen. Consider placing flowers before the statue or image of Mary after the ceremony has ended. It is most appropriate if the bride and groom do this together—a good symbol of their newly sealed relationship as a couple. After you place the flowers before the Virgin Mary, spend a brief time in prayer, asking Mary to intercede for you and to bless your Marriage. However, if devotion to Mary is not an important part of your personal prayer life, this ritual would not have much meaning and would not be appropriate to include at your wedding.

31. How do we know what music to choose?

Early on in the preparation process (once you have the date confirmed at the parish where you will be celebrating your wedding), make an appointment to meet with the parish music director. If your parish does not have a music director, ask the priest or wedding coordinator what the parish policies are regarding music, and who will be playing for your wedding. In many parishes, you must use the parish musician. In others, you are encouraged or even required to find your own musician. You need to find out the policy of the parish first, and then proceed from there.

Regarding the choice of music: the musician with whom you meet should be able to make recommendations. Some musicians provide a CD of the various pieces that are commonly used for weddings in the parish or the musician might direct you to a website in which you can listen to various options. Other musicians may play selections from which you can choose. Keep in mind that the music for your wedding should be sung and played live. Prerecorded music is not allowed in Catholic liturgy.

If there is a piece of music you would especially like to have played or sung at your wedding, bring it to the musician for consideration. Church musicians are guided by certain Church documents and policies. Your musician or music director can advise you about appropriate choices, and also provide some very good choices with which you may not be familiar. Come to the meeting with an open mind and a willingness to hear new music that would be beautiful and appropriate for your wedding ceremony.

32. Do we have to use the church musicians? Our cousin sings and can do the solos.

Ideally, any singer at your wedding would be familiar with Catholic rituals and have some understanding of the role of a cantor, psalmist, or soloist at such a ceremony. You will need a singer to lead everyone in singing the Responsorial Psalm (whether you are celebrating with or without a Mass) and the various acclamations of the Mass (Holy, Holy, Holy; Memorial Acclamation; Amen; and Lamb of God). Solos may be sung before the ceremony begins, during the Preparation of the Gifts, and/or after Communion, but a soloist should not be the only one singing the parts of the ceremony that are intended for the participation of everyone. This is where a worship aid can be of great help.

Keep these considerations in mind when asking someone to sing at your wedding. Is your cousin (friend, aunt, sister, and so on) familiar with the Roman Catholic rituals, and does he or she understand the role of a cantor or psalmist? It is usually wiser to hire musicians through the parish where you will be married. However, if your cousin (or friend, or other relative) really wants to sing at your wedding and has a truly beautiful voice—as well as lots of experience singing in public situations—you might consider this: hire a parish cantor to serve as cantor (leading the singing of the assembly) and psalmist (singing the Responsorial Psalm), and have your relative/ friend sing a solo during the Preparation of the Gifts, or as a prelude before the wedding ceremony begins. Remember that whatever they sing will need to follow Church and diocesan guidelines regarding choice of music, and will most likely need to be approved by the music director or organist (and sometimes by the presiding priest). This way, your relative/friend would not be placed into an unfamiliar situation, but they can still contribute to the beauty and prayerfulness of your wedding.

Keep in mind that some churches require that you use their musicians. If you wish to use other musicians, you may still be required to pay the church musician a fee.

Any music at your wedding is always at the service of the Catholic ritual. The music chosen to be sung or played at your wedding needs to enhance the prayer of all those gathered to celebrate, first and foremost. A lovely solo is very nice, but if it distracts from and does not contribute to the prayerfulness of the occasion, it is not appropriate to be sung.

33. We love the song "From This Moment On" by Shania Twain. It's a perfect wedding song! Can we have it sung at our wedding?

When you meet with the musician and select the music for your wedding ceremony, one of the things to remember is that you are celebrating the Sacrament of Matrimony within a Catholic liturgy, which is the public prayer of the Church. There are three principles used by Catholic Church musicians when choosing music for a Mass or any other liturgy: pastoral, liturgical, and musical. The same principles are to be used when choosing music for Sunday Mass, a wedding, a funeral, or any other sacramental celebration. What do these principles tell us?

Pastoral: Is the music appropriate for this particular community and this particular celebration? Does it have the capability of drawing the gathered assembly closer to the sacred mysteries being celebrated?

Liturgical: Does the music being considered fit within the liturgy being celebrated? Does it express our belief in God/Jesus Christ, and does it fit at this particular time of the Mass? (For example, a Communion song might not be appropriate as a processional song, nor would a love song that makes no mention of Jesus or the love of God be appropriate at a wedding liturgy.)

Musical: Is it good music? Can this particular musical selection bear the weight of the sacredness of the occasion? Is it artistically sound and worthy of the mysteries being celebrated?

If you are considering a "popular" song for your wedding, look at the lyrics (words) and the style of the music and ask yourself if this particular song will help people pray at your wedding and help you and everyone else present be in touch with the sacredness of the occasion. Would this song be appropriate at a Sunday liturgy? If not, it would be far preferable to include the song in the music at the reception after the wedding ceremony.

A great source of songs for your sacramental wedding ceremony is the parish hymnal. Do you have any favorite hymns or songs that would express the love that the two of you share for God? If you will celebrate with a Mass, what is your favorite Communion song? Are there other songs in the parish repertoire that you especially like and that would fit in the liturgy of your wedding ceremony? When you go to Mass on Sunday, look for songs that might be appropriate for your wedding and discuss them with the musician.

34. Can our sister sing "Ave Maria" as a Communion meditation song at our wedding? It is a Church song.

There are three concerns regarding the singing of the "Ave Maria" after Communion. First, any music sung during or immediately following Communion should be sung by the whole community.[12] However, if

---

12 See *Sing to the Lord: Music in Divine Worship*, 189.

the Communion procession goes on for a long time—which is usually not the case at a wedding—it is permissible to combine music for the congregation and music for the choir alone. Second, the silent time of prayer after Communion is important. Processing forward and receiving Communion is a public act of worship, but many people treasure the few minutes of silence allowed and encouraged to take place after everyone has received Communion. There is no mention in any Church documents for a solo to be sung after Communion. Third, the song that is chosen for this time should focus on the mystery of Holy Communion.[13] What this tells us is that in addition to the post-Communion song being a song for the assembly, it should also be liturgically suitable for this time of the Mass, in other words, it should have some relationship to what we have just done—received the Body and Blood of Christ. The "Ave Maria," or other Marian hymns, do not relate directly to the fact that we have all just shared in the Body and Blood of Christ. Consider using Marian hymns as a musical prelude before your ceremony begins, either as a solo, sung by a choir or small ensemble, or instrumentally. If it is the practice in your parish for brides or couples to place flowers and pray before a statue or image of the Blessed Virgin Mary, this would be an appropriate time for the "Ave Maria." At this point in the liturgy, it can be sung by a soloist. It is best to check with your parish staff about this option.[14]

35. We thought that we could use the "Wedding March" as our instrumental for the opening procession, but we were told it's not allowed. We don't understand why because everyone uses this piece at weddings.

First, a clarification: there are two compositions that have come to be called the "Wedding March." The first is Richard Wagner's "Bridal Chorus" from the opera *Lohengrin*, often requested for the opening

---

13 See *Sing to the Lord: Music in Divine Worship*, 196.
14 Refer to question 30 on page 56.

procession. (You know . . . "Here comes the bride . . .") The second is "The Wedding March" by Felix Mendelssohn. It is often used at the end of weddings, as the bride and groom process out of the church.

Mendelssohn's "Wedding March" is one of the best known pieces from his suite of incidental music for the Shakespearean play, *A Midsummer Night's Dream*. The play is a comedy portraying the wedding of the Duke of Athens (Theseus) and the Amazon queen Hippolyta. The play is filled with the shenanigans of characters who are manipulated by fairies and carry on in all sorts of ways. Richard Wagner's "Bridal Chorus" is from the opera *Lohengrin,* and is sung by the women of the wedding party as they accompany the bride, Elsa, to the bridal chamber. Both of these pieces are considered secular music.

In question 33 we covered the three judgments offered as criteria for music to be used in a Catholic liturgy: liturgical, pastoral, and musical.[15] If you hold both of these pieces up to the scrutiny of these three judgments, both of them would fail. While they are well-written compositions by noted composers, they do not stand up to the pastoral and liturgical judgments. The circumstance for which the music was written does not contribute to a reverent or sacred understanding of Marriage. Thus, most Roman Catholic parishes or dioceses forbid (or at least discourage) the use of these musical compositions.

There are numerous other pieces—pieces written specifically to be played in church—that would be suitable and that would convey the joy and beauty of your wedding. When you meet with the music director of the parish, or the person who will be playing instrument(s) at your wedding, I am sure they will have other musical selections to recommend. Hopefully you will find something far more appropriate in keeping with the sacredness and dignity of your Marriage celebration in the Catholic Church.

---

15 See question 33 on page 59 for a more detailed explanation of these criteria.

36. Can we have a theme Mass where all the music is from our favorite Disney movie?

In short, the answer is no. As mentioned above, any music at your wedding liturgy needs to have some relevance to the sacredness of the event, be reflective of your love for God, and also be appropriate to the liturgical action that is taking place; therefore, you may not use Disney music (or other secular music) during your wedding liturgy.

The reception is a more appropriate place to play or perform music that does not meet the requirements of the Catholic liturgy. When you choose to celebrate the Sacrament of Matrimony in the Catholic Church, you implicitly agree to follow the liturgical norms of the Church and to strive for a ceremony that clearly expresses the sacredness of your Marriage in a reverent, dignified, and prayerful way. Any music that does not contribute to those norms should be saved for the party afterward!

37. Can we have photos or video taken in the church during the Mass? In the church after the Mass? Are there any guidelines we need to give our videographer and photographer?

Most parishes have guidelines regarding photography and videography, so be sure to ask. The guidelines are to not make your life or the life of your photographer difficult. They are to preserve the sacredness and dignity of the celebration of the sacrament of your Marriage. The uppermost concern is that everyone is able to pray and enter into the ritual with as little distraction as possible. (This policy goes for your guests as well. Have you ever sat behind or near someone in church who is constantly taking pictures? It is really distracting and can be annoying to many people.)

There are also concerns about where the photographer will stand, or from where he or she can take photographs, as well as the use of flash photography. While the photographer wants to get the best pictures possible for your wedding album, your priest and anyone from the parish staff who is working with you is most concerned that your wedding will be a prayerful and dignified experience for everyone, without the distraction of camera flashes and a photographer walking all around the sanctuary or in front of guests to get the best shots.

Your parish will probably provide you with guidelines, which you really need to share with your photographer and videographer. To prevent uncomfortable situations, it is best to get the written guidelines from the parish and share them with your photographer and/or videographer well before the wedding so that everyone understands their boundaries. Always keep in mind that the purpose of such guidelines is not to restrict the professionals you hire, but to preserve the dignity and prayerfulness of your celebration.

38. Do we need to have a program for our wedding? What should the program include?

Many couples like to create a keepsake program with the names of the people in the wedding party and other pertinent information. However, it would be much more helpful to your guests if you provided a program that is a true *worship aid*, something which would help your guests participate in the singing and the verbal responses of the prayers. The music and words of songs could be included, or even just a reference to the page number in the hymnal or worship aid resource that is in the pews. It would be hospitable to include spoken responses for the various dialogues that take place between priest and people, particularly if you have guests who are not Catholic. If there is already something in the pews with the responses, a simple reference to those books or cards could be included in your program.

When you celebrate your wedding in the Catholic Church, one of the principles to remember is the importance of participation by everyone present. Catholic rituals are participative. We are all supposed to sing, respond, and say the various prayers out loud. While this does not always happen at weddings, it is important for you, as the bride and groom, to help encourage that participation as much as possible. One of the ways you can do that is by planning for and providing a program that will help people participate. The musician for your wedding or the parish wedding coordinator should be able to help you with this, using music that at least some of your guests would know and be able to sing. It is also very helpful to include the spoken responses to the greetings and prayers of the priest or deacon for the benefit of those who are not familiar with the Catholic liturgy. The musician or wedding coordinator may have some samples and/or templates that you can use to create your own program, which will enable and encourage your guests to fully participate in the prayers and songs of your wedding celebration. Your wedding can be so much more joyful when your guests join in the singing and prayer responses!

39. The florist would like us to purchase an aisle runner for our wedding. May we use runners in the church?

When you receive your wedding guidelines from the parish, check to see if there are restrictions about aisle runners. Most of the time, when a parish does not permit the use of an aisle runner it is for practical reasons. Plastic aisle runners can create a slippery surface, which could be dangerous as you walk down the aisle (especially in churches that have marble floors). The unrolling of an aisle runner right before the bride enters may disrupt the procession or even give undue emphasis to the entrance of the bride rather than the unity of the couple.[16] Some parishes do not permit aisle runners because the main aisle is carpeted and slopes toward the altar area. Use of a runner in that or many other places could create a potentially dangerous situation.

---

16 See also question 12.

40. We would like to put flowers (or bows) at the ends of all the pews for our wedding to make the church look festive. Can we do that?

You will need to check with the parish or look in the wedding guidelines for the answer to your question because policies differ from parish to parish.

One word of caution: if you choose to place flowers or bows at the ends of the pews, find out how the florist plans to attach them. Ask the florist to use elastic bands or some type of ribbon that can be wrapped around the tops of the pews. Church pews are usually made of wood—similar to the fine furniture in your home. Pins, thumbtacks, or tape can damage the wood. Always treat the furnishings and other appointments in the church as you would any fine furniture or décor in your own home, or in your friend's home.

Also keep in mind that parishes do have rules for where flowers can be placed. The placement of the flowers needs to be considered so that the flowers don't get in the way of the ritual action or overpower the main symbols of the liturgy. You may put flowers in front of the ambo (the place where the readings are proclaimed) or on either side of the altar. Because the altar is a primary symbol of Christ in the liturgy, flowers may not be placed on top of the altar or be so big that the symbolism of the altar is obscured. Be sure to consult with the wedding coordinator at your parish. Oftentimes, the church is already decorated to enhance the liturgical season. Many parishes ask that the seasonal environment remain in its place during your wedding liturgy. The season should be reflected environmentally in whatever is taking place in the church, including weddings. And for practical purposes, it is very difficult for parish staffs to be expected to take down seasonal decorations in time for a wedding only to replace these decorations in time for the weekend liturgies, which are the most important liturgies of the Christian week (the Sunday celebration of the Mass).

41. Do you recommend having a receiving line at the Church immediately after the wedding?

A receiving line is a lovely way to greet all your guests and introduce family members to your new spouse. For practical reasons, it might not be best to have one at the church. Many churches have multiple weddings on weekends, or their regular Saturday evening Mass or even Saturday confessions are scheduled after the wedding ceremony concludes. For these reasons, if you are going to have a receiving line, it is far more reasonable and practical to have the receiving line at the place of your reception. If you celebrate your Marriage at a regularly scheduled Sunday (or Saturday) parish Mass, perhaps you could have the receiving line in the parish hall or somewhere else on parish property so as not to interfere with people coming for the next Mass.

42. May we throw bird seed or rice, or blow bubbles after the ceremony?

Catholic parishes in the United States have different policies regarding the throwing of rice or bird seed, or the blowing of bubbles. Keep in mind that seeds and grains of rice can create a safety hazard for people coming into the church for Masses or other events that take place after your wedding. They can also be a health hazard for birds that swallow them. Even bubbles can cause problems on certain surfaces and can be toxic to wildlife. In addition, many parishes do not have maintenance staff on duty on weekends, so sweeping and cleaning up such things would not be done until Monday morning, leaving the remnants of you wedding on the steps or ground in front of the church for weekend liturgies.

It is best to consult the parish about this and comply with whatever policies they have in place, but ultimately it is important to respect the space of the church.

43. Why do we have to pay for use of the church and give the priest or deacon a stipend?

There are many costs involved in most weddings. Common expenses include those of a reception venue, caterer, musicians, decorations, flowers, photographer, and so on. All of these are considered normal expenses and most couples pay them without question. What you pay all these "vendors" covers the costs of materials that are used, maintenance and utility costs for the building, the salaries of those working for you, and numerous other expenses.

Churches, just like businesses, have overhead expenses. Lighting, heating, cooling, and other electrical costs are incurred when the church building is used for your rehearsal and wedding. Candles and other liturgical supplies are expensive. Before your wedding, a lot of paperwork must be processed by someone on the parish staff. After the wedding, someone usually needs to clean up the rooms used by the bridal party.

Likewise, the priest or deacon will spend considerable time meeting with you and preparing for your wedding ceremony (homilies take time to prepare!). It is customary and considerate to offer the clergyman a stipend for the time and effort he puts into preparing for your wedding. It is time taken away from other parish or personal responsibilities. In parishes with which I am familiar, the stipend for the priest or deacon is not required. It is really a gesture of gratitude from the bride and groom or their parents. It would also be a kind gesture to offer a small stipend to altar servers, who are usually giving up time on a weekend to serve at your wedding.

When you compare what the parish is charging with what you pay for your wedding reception, dress, photography, and other items, the parish fees are most likely a small percentage of all the other expenses.

44. Can we hire a wedding coordinator to take care of the ceremony for us?

When you hire a professional wedding coordinator, usually they are not familiar with the Catholic wedding ceremony or the policies of the particular parish church. Their concern is to carry out your wishes regarding the flow of the day and the various aspects of the reception. A professional wedding coordinator is not the person to put in charge of what takes place in the church.

Many parishes have a person in charge of wedding ceremonies who works with the couple. This representative of the parish understands the Catholic ritual and will work with you in making your wedding ceremony as beautiful and prayerful as possible. She or he is also familiar with the church facility and knows how to prepare the church for your ceremony, whether it is a Mass or Liturgy of the Word.

You will be in good hands with the parish wedding coordinator, priest, or whomever it is in the parish that does the immediate preparations for weddings.

45. The process of engagement and the many details of preparing the wedding ceremony and the reception are very time consuming and stressful. How can we maintain a spirit of prayer throughout the process and keep ourselves focused on what's important: the Sacrament of Matrimony?

As your wedding date gets closer, you two will get busier and busier with all the details of preparing your big day. There will be many things demanding your attention, and many decisions will need to be made by the two of you. Are you managing to keep yourselves grounded in what is really important to you? Are you keeping open the lines of communication and treating each other with love, respect, and honor? Are you trying your best to stay close to God—to spend time together in prayer, even if only participating in Mass every

Sunday and praying together before meals (and perhaps before you go your separate ways after spending time together)?

Your wedding day is important. But even more important are the years of Marriage that follow, the day-to-day decisions to love each other "for better or for worse." Five years from now—maybe even just one or two years from now, you won't remember all the little details that didn't go quite right, the glitches that most of your guests won't even know about at all.

If you can develop good habits now of praying together and respecting each other's opinions and feelings, those good habits have the potential to last many years and to enrich and strengthen your relationship with each other. There will be some things on your wedding day that are totally out of your control, but the less you fret about them the more joyful your day will be.

What is important on your wedding day is that you celebrate a sacred occasion, the sacrament of your Marriage among loving family and friends, supported by their prayer and blessing and that of the Church. You are looking forward to a long life together, and the blessing of children borne out of your love for one another. What is important now is that you maintain your loving relationship with each other and with God. The dress will be put away, the flowers will fade, but your love for each other and your faith in God will endure and will carry you through many years of a happy and fruitful Marriage. That's really what this is all about, isn't it? In the words of Pope Francis:

> It is good that your wedding be simple and make what is truly important stand out. Some are more concerned with the exterior details; with the banquet, the photographs, the clothes, the flowers . . . These are important for a celebration, but only if they point to the real reason for your joy: the Lord's blessing on your love.[17]

Finally, as you continue with the preparations for your Marriage, you may wish to ask your parents or the priest or deacon with whom

---

17 Address to engaged couples in Rome, February 14, 2014.

you are working to bless the two of you with this lovely prayer. It is a fitting prayer to use at frequent times during your engagement.

We give you praise, O Lord,
who in your gentle wisdom call and prepare
your son and daughter **N.** and **N.**
to love each other.
Graciously strengthen their hearts, we pray,
so that, by keeping faith and pleasing you in all things,
they may come happily to the Sacrament of Marriage.
Through Christ our Lord.
R. Amen.[18]

---

18 This prayer is an excerpt from the Order for the Blessing of an Engaged Couple. A longer service exists. If you wish for a longer blessing, consult your pastor or liturgist.

Index